Soul Wounds for Fatherless Daughters

The Echoes of Absence.
A Healing Journey for Fatherless Daughters

Dear Beautiful Soul,

Sometimes, we may not have been able to converse honestly with our fathers for various reasons. We were afraid to ask some questions, and some they either declined to answer or simply were not present. Safe spaces may not have been created due to emotional unavailability or various insecurities. Unanswered questions, their lack of presence or emotional unavailability can often leave us feeling stuck.

Healing a "father" wound is essential for several reasons. It allows us to confront, heal, and understand the emotional pain that may have stemmed from those experiences. Acknowledging their existence, whether these wounds are abandonment, injustice, betrayal, rejection, or humiliation, is the first step to healing.

This journal was created with compassion for wounded fatherless daughters, whether adopted or raised by another masculine energy. Welcome to your safe place. You were brave enough to take the journey. Remember to be kind to yourself throughout this process.

Remember that healing is a process, and it is not linear. Take as many breaks as often as needed if things get too emotional. It's your journey. You got this!

Publisher Awareherness Press Publishers
Awareherness@gmail.com

ISBN 978-1-965702-04-8

IV

Unpacking
Your Heart

Day 1

Reflecting on the term "father wound," what does it mean to you?

....
....
....
....
....
....
....
....
....
....
....
....
....
....
....
....
....

Day 2

What feelings surface When you think about your father?

....

....

....

....

....

....

....

....

....

....

....

....

....

....

....

....

....

05

Day 3

If you've never met your father, imagine what he would be like. Describe what you envisioned.

....

....

....

....

....

....

....

....

....

....

....

....

....

....

....

....

....

Day 4

Describe the moment you met your father.

....
....
....
....
....
....
....
....
....
....
....
....
....
....
....
....
....
....

Day 5

What age did you meet your father? What was your first thought when you met him?

....

....

....

....

....

....

....

....

....

....

....

....

....

....

....

....

Day 6

Describe the moment your father left.

....
....
....
- -
- -
- -
- -
- -
- -
- -
- -
- -
- -
- -
- -

Day 7

How has his absence affected your life?

....
....
....
....
....
....
....
....
....
....
....
....
....
....
....
....
....

Day 8

What lessons have you learned from your father's absence?

....
....
....
....
....
....
....
....
....
....
....
....
....
....
....
....

Day 9

Do you believe that his absence has affected your relationships in your life?

....

....

....

....

....

....

....

....

....

....

....

....

....

....

....

....

Day 10

Writing can be therapeutic. Compose a letter to your younger self discussing your relationship with your father. Discuss how you can work through your wound of betrayal, rejection, and abandonment.

Embracing
Forgiveness

Day 11

How do you view men or father figures in your life?

....

....

....

....

....

....

....

....

....

....

....

....

....

....

....

....

....

....

....

....

Day 12

How do you feel towards others who reject or abandon you?

....

....

....

....

....

....

....

....

....

....

....

....

....

....

....

....

....

....

Day 13

What does forgiveness mean to you?

....
....
....
....
....
....
....
....
....
....
....
....
....
....
....
....
....
....

Day 14

Have you forgiven your father?

....
....
....
....
....
....
....
....
....
....
....
....
....
....
....
....
....
....

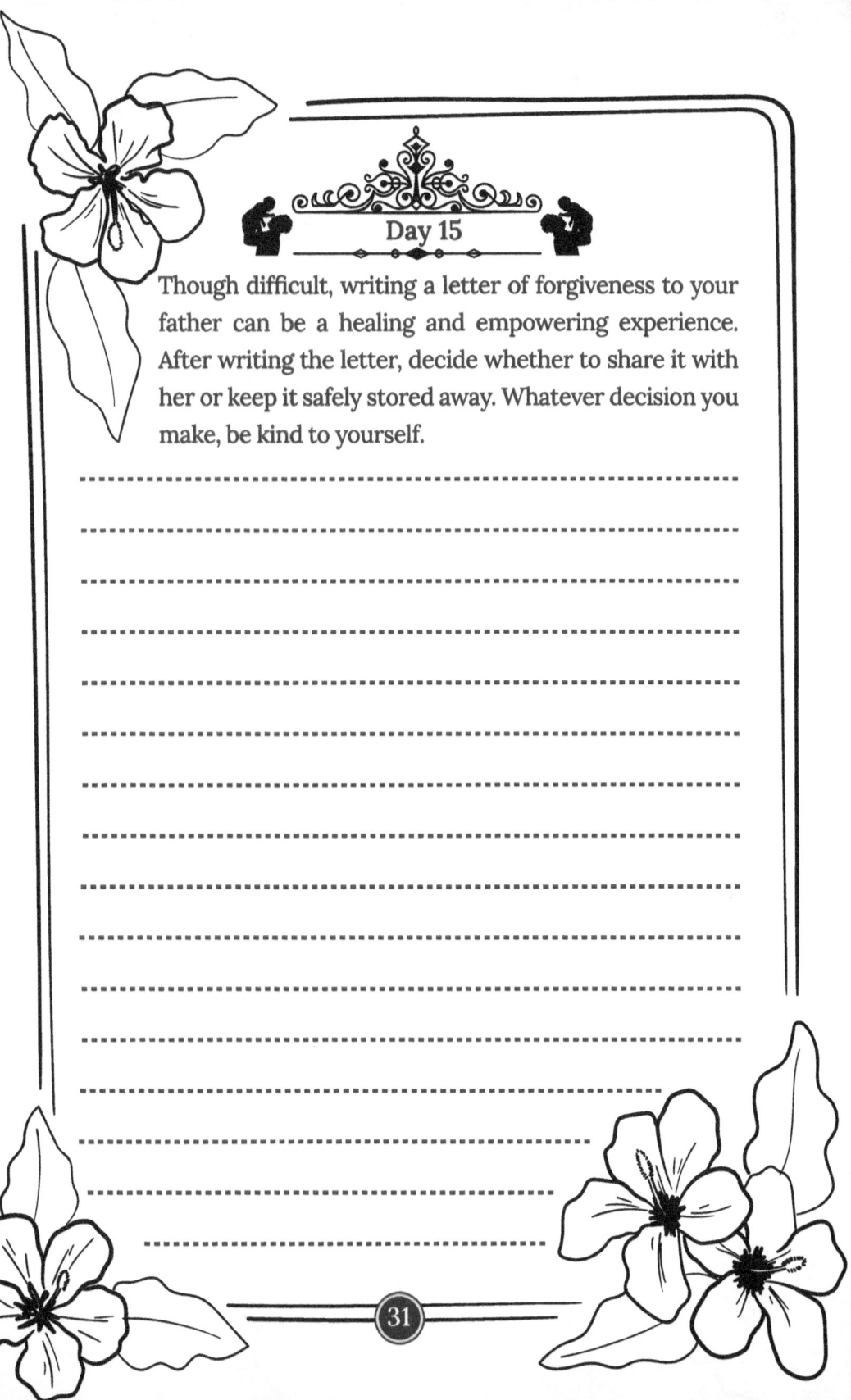

Day 15

Though difficult, writing a letter of forgiveness to your father can be a healing and empowering experience. After writing the letter, decide whether to share it with her or keep it safely stored away. Whatever decision you make, be kind to yourself.

Day 16

Describe a moment when your father added joy to your life.

....

....

....

....

....

....

....

....

....

....

....

....

....

....

....

....

....

Day 17

Do you trust your father since he entered your life?

....
....
....
....
....
....
....
....
....
....
....
....
....
....
....
....
....
....
....

Day 18

Are there any feelings concerning forming a safe relationship with your father?

....

....

....

....

....

....

....

....

....

....

....

....

....

....

....

....

....

....

Day 19

What do you wish you could tell your father about your feelings? Write down how you feel.

....
....
....
....
....
....
....
....
....
....
....
....
....
....
....

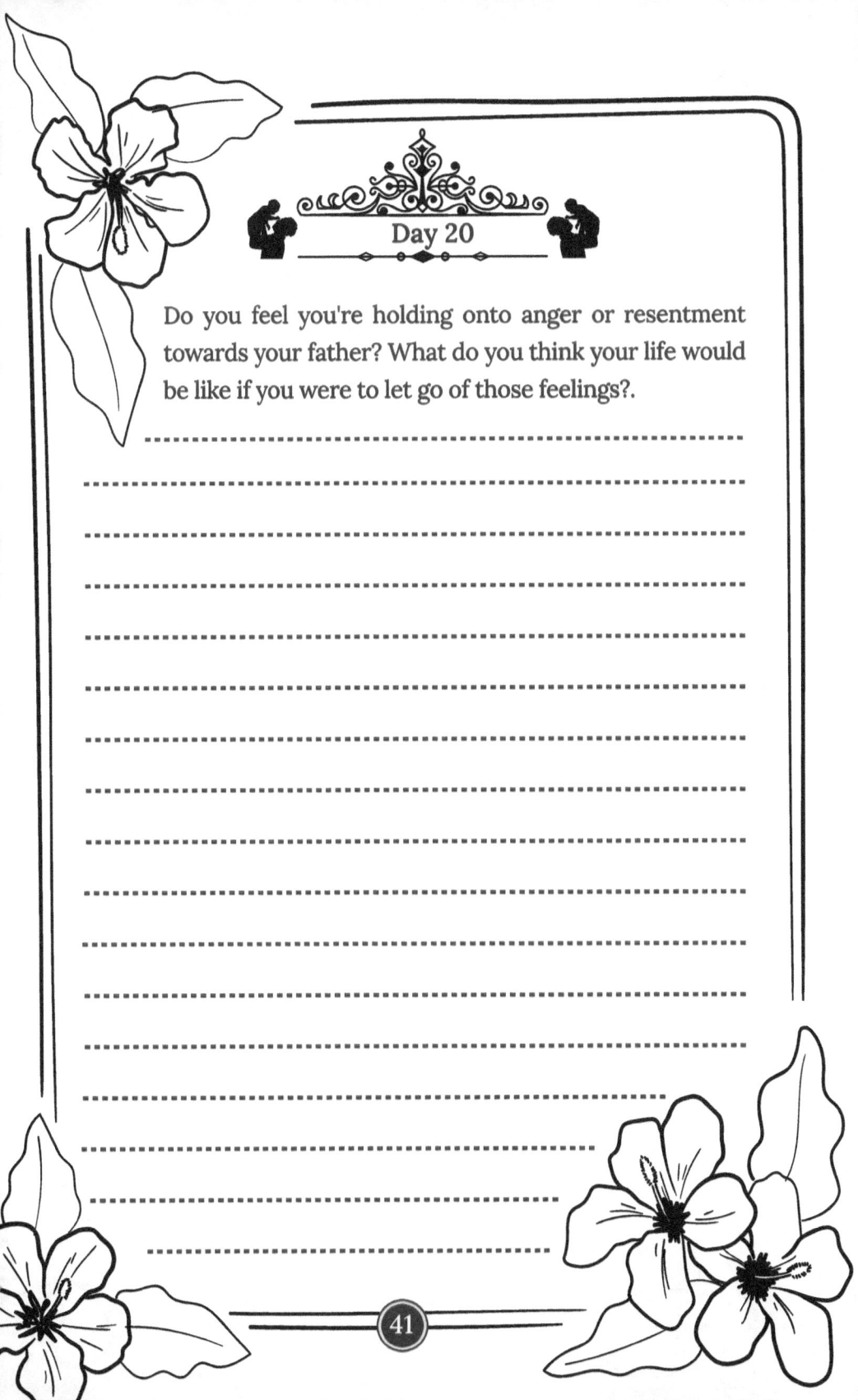

Day 20

Do you feel you're holding onto anger or resentment towards your father? What do you think your life would be like if you were to let go of those feelings?.

Navigating
Your Emotions

Day 21

Do you blame yourself for your father leaving?

....
....
....
....
....
....
....
....
....
....
....
....
....
....
....
....
....
....
....

Day 22

If your father were to come back into your life, would you welcome him positively? Please describe your response, whether it's yes or no.

Day 23

How did your mom or family explain your father's absence? Were they truthful?

....

....

....

....

....

....

....

....

....

....

....

....

....

....

....

....

....

Day 24

Do you believe that your father's actions have affected your self-worth? Describe how they have affected you.

....
....
....
....
....
....
....
....
....
....
....
....
....
....
....
....

Day 25

Our father's actions may have sometimes impacted our self-esteem. Write down how you feel without critical judgment toward yourself.

Day 26

Were you a daddy's girl? How would you describe your relationship now?

....

....

....

....

....

....

....

....

....

....

....

....

....

....

....

Day 27

How can you honor your feelings while navigating your emotions toward forgiveness?

....
....
....
....
....
....
....
....
....
....
....
....
....
....
....
....

Day 28

Are you ready to let go and move on without your father's presence?

....
....
....
....
....
....
....
....
....
....
....
....
....
....
....
....
....

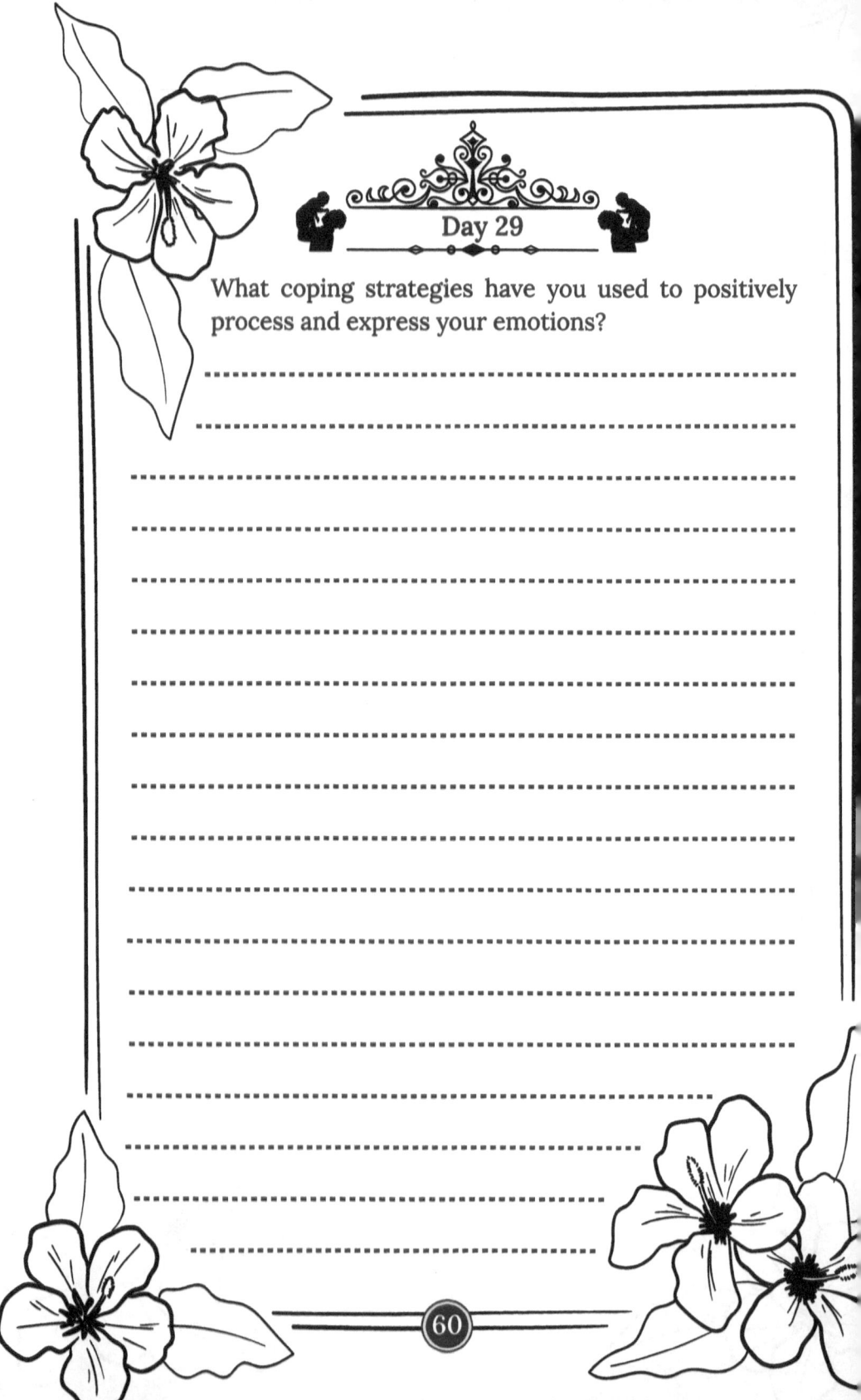

Day 29

What coping strategies have you used to positively process and express your emotions?

....
....
....
....
....
....
....
....
....
....
....
....
....
....
....
....

Day 30

What triggers these emotions, and how are you healthily managing them?

....
....
....
....
....
....
....
....
....
....
....
....
....
....
....
....

Finding Peace
Through Healing

Day 31

What self-care practices have you chosen today to promote healing from emotional wounds?

....
....
....
....
....
....
....
....
....
....
....
....
....
....
....
....
....
....

Day 32

Describe a self-care routine that brings you peace and comfort. If you haven't developed one, create one here.

Day 33

How do you nurture your inner child to heal through the wounds of rejection, abandonment, betrayal, injustice, and humiliation?

....
....
....
....
....
....
....
....
....
....
....
....
....
....
....

Day 34

Name five mindfulness practices that help cope with emotions. How have you found them helpful?

....

....

....

....

....

....

....

....

....

....

....

....

....

....

....

....

....

....

Day 35

Healing can be enjoyable. Create a vision board for your healing journey.

....

....

....

....

....

....

....

....

....

....

....

....

....

....

....

....

....

....

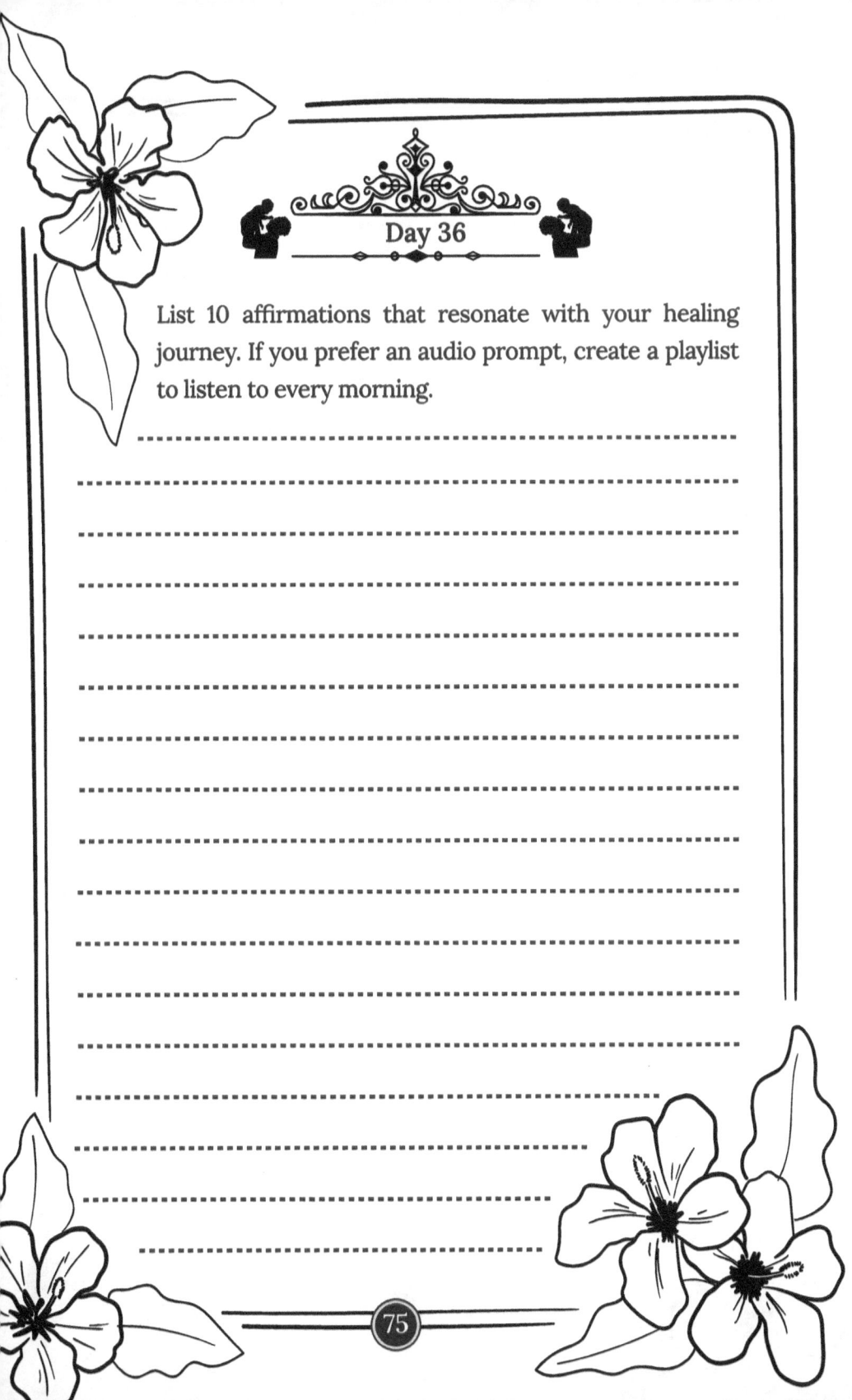

Day 36

List 10 affirmations that resonate with your healing journey. If you prefer an audio prompt, create a playlist to listen to every morning.

Day 37

What hobbies bring you joy? How can you incorporate them into your routine?

....

....

....

....

....

....

....

....

....

....

....

....

....

....

....

....

....

Day 38

Reflect on the significance of support systems in the healing process and identify your support network.

....

....

....

....

....

....

....

....

....

....

....

....

....

....

....

....

....

Day 39

Write about a book or resource that has helped you understand your feelings.

....
....
....
....
....
....
....
....
....
....
....
....
....
....
....
....

Day 40

Try a new activity that feels nurturing (e.g., yoga, art). Reflect on the experience.

Embracing
Change

Day 41

If you are a single mom, have you shared your fatherless experience with your child?

....

....

....

....

....

....

....

....

....

....

....

....

....

....

....

....

....

Day 42

How do you want your relationship with your father to evolve?

....
....
....
....
....
....
....
....
....
....
....
....
....
....
....
....
....

Day 43

Write about how you can communicate your needs more effectively.

Day 44

If you are a single mom, write about the qualities you want to embody.

....

....

....

....

....

....

....

....

....

....

....

....

....

....

....

....

Day 45

Describe your hopes for the future of your father-daughter relationship.

....

....

....

....

....

....

....

....

....

....

....

....

....

....

....

....

Day 46

What would you like to say to your father in a future conversation? What prevents the conversation from happening?

....

....

....

....

....

....

....

....

....

....

....

....

....

....

....

Day 47

Are you the generational curse breaker? What do you want to change?

....

....

....

....

....

....

....

....

....

....

....

....

....

....

....

....

Day 48

Write a letter to your future self about your healing journey. Re-visit it every day for encouragement.

....
....
....
....
....
....
....
....
....
....
....
....
....
....
....
....
....

Day 49

Great or small, what positive changes have you noticed in yourself during this process?

....

....

....

....

....

....

....

....

....

....

....

....

....

....

....

....

Day 49

Create a list of goals for your emotional well-being moving forward.

Reflections
of Gratitude

Day 51

Reflecting on your journey so far. Where do you see the most significant area of improvement?

....

....

....

....

....

....

....

....

....

....

....

....

....

....

....

....

....

Day 52

Write about the most significant change you've experienced while on this 60-day journal.

....

....

....

....

....

....

....

....

....

....

....

....

....

....

....

....

....

....

Day 53

List three things you are grateful for in your relationship or the time spent with your father.

....

....

....

....

....

....

....

....

....

....

....

....

....

....

....

....

....

Day 54

Describe a recent moment of connection with your father. Has it improved since your journey began?

....

....

....

....

....

....

....

....

....

....

....

....

....

....

....

....

....

....

....

Day 55

How have your perceptions of your men changed since the day of journaling?

....
....
....
....
....
....
....
....
....
....
....
....
....
....
....
....
....
....

Day 56

Write about how you can continue to nurture your healing process beyond your journey.

....

....

....

....

....

....

....

....

....

....

....

....

....

....

....

....

Day 57

Have you identified what support you need moving forward? What does that look like to you?

....

....

....

....

....

....

....

....

....

....

....

....

....

....

....

....

....

Day 58

Reflect on how this journey has impacted your self-identity.

....
....
....
....
....
....
....
....
....
....
....
....
....
....
....
....
....
....

Day 59

Write your father a letter of love and appreciation.

....
....
....
....
....
....
....
....
....
....
....
....
....
....
....
....
....
....
....
....

Day 60

Celebrate your journey! What are your takeaways, and how will you continue to.

....
....
....
....
....
....
....
....
....
....
....
....
....
....
....
....
....
....

Congratulations on Your Journey!

Congratulations on completing this healing journal. Reflecting on your relationship concerning your absent father and any resulting wounds is a significant accomplishment.

Over the past sixty days, you've courageously faced your emotions, recognized your experiences, and embraced the healing journey. Every prompt, reflection, and exercise has contributed to your self-discovery and growth.

As you finish this chapter, remember that healing is a continuous journey. The knowledge and lessons you have gained will continue to influence your path ahead. Embrace the strength you have developed and carry it with you as you transition into your next phase of life.

Celebrate your resilience, honor your progress, and recognize the bravery it takes to confront your wounds. You are worthy of love, healing, and a future filled with possibilities.

Thank you for allowing this journal to be a part of your journey. May you nurture your spirit and cultivate healing in all areas of your life.

With heartfelt congratulations,

Dr. Kellie Diane